Praise fo

"When I want the best, I go to Noven Jaisi."
Michael Lloyd, *Grammy-winning producer*

"I cannot fathom just how gifted Noven Jaisi is.
His heartfelt talents are so beautifully expressed
in all that he creates. I am his biggest fan!"
Mike Love, *lead singer of The Beach Boys*

"Noven Jaisi has the power to captivate *anyone*.
He is a true visionary."
Dr. Harjit Sidhu, Ph.D.

"What incredible work!"
Leif Garret

"Noven Jaisi is a genius."
John Stamos

NOVEN JAISI

MAKE
HISTORY

HOW TO MAKE THE MOST
OF YOUR TIME ON EARTH

NOVEN JAISI

MAKE
HISTORY

HOW TO MAKE THE MOST
OF YOUR TIME ON EARTH

Make History

Published by: Noven Jaisi Company
(Kuala Lumpur, Malaysia)

ISBN: 978-967-26951-0-3

ISBN (eBook): 978-967-26951-1-0

First Edition

The author had made best efforts to determine the sources of all quotes contained herein.

To those who are committed to growth.

WARNING

THE TEACHINGS IN THIS BOOK ARE NOT FOR THE FAINT-HEARTED—NOR FOR ANYONE WITH A RIGID MINDSET. THIS BOOK IS FOR INDIVIDUALS WHO ARE COMMITTED TO BECOMING THE GREATEST VERSION OF THEMSELVES. IT'S FOR THOSE WHO ARE WILLING TO DO WHATEVER IT TAKES TO ATTAIN THE QUALITY OF LIFE THEY'RE AFTER. IF THAT'S NOT YOU, **DO NOT READ THIS BOOK.**

Honestly, if you're not committed,
STOP HERE.

COMMITMENT CONTRACT

I, _____, have hereby chosen of my own volition to read the book *Make History*. I understand that the information in this book has been carefully researched, and all efforts have been made to ensure results. Thus, I hereby declare that I will participate in each activity included. I will also experiment with every strategy presented. I hereby resolve that post-reading, I will be committed to doing whatever it takes to attain the quality of life I desire. I will be receptive. I will not make excuses. I will not settle. I will not blame anyone (or anything). I will take action.

_____   _____

Signature   **Date**

Contents

Preface

I t was New Year's Eve 2013, and I was crafting a to-do list that comprised all the steps I needed to take as I embarked on the beginning of a new chapter of my life: my first full-time job.

It wasn't just any job. It was the job I desired most at the time: chief video editor. Although I was twenty years old, which is fairly young for the position, the owner of the company believed in me and was insistent that I accept his generous offer. On top of a lucrative contract, I was also promised carte blanche in terms of all creative aspects, which is an absolute rarity. It was the culmination of seven years of hard work finally paying off. I was *beyond* thrilled.

It was only a few weeks later that I would find myself in the psychiatric unit in University Malaya Hospital, diagnosed with bipolar disorder.

My condition was the result of poor life choices that snowballed over time. Back then, I completely neglected my physical and mental health. I viewed the world in a way that didn't serve me. I also had a myriad of disempowering beliefs. All of this led me to a very dark place mentally, and to deal with it—I turned to drugs.

My drug addiction, along with my erratic sleeping pattern and my pessimistic outlook on life, all aided in triggering my mental illness. The illness was so severe that it was apparent to anyone who interacted with me. I was unable to have a conversation with someone without alarming them; there was no hiding it.

My symptoms included racing thoughts, hallucinations, rapid speech, delusions, paranoia, and severe insomnia. To put it simply: *my brain was on fire*. Things were bleak, and everyone, including the doctor who treated me, made it clear that my condition was incurable.

The illness led to a series of episodes that put me and the people around me in danger, many of which I have little or no memory of. One of them included me ramming my car repeatedly into another car in traffic. I have no idea why I did it, but it happened. Thankfully, no one was injured, and I'm also lucky that the driver in the other car was understanding of my condition.

Worst of all was what I had put my family through; I can only imagine what it must have felt like for them. We weren't well informed on mental health, nor did we have anyone in the family who had gone through anything similar; it was all very foreign to us.

Not only did this leave me unemployed and in financial ruin, but it also left me completely *lost*. I had absolutely no idea what I wanted to do with my life. I was at rock bottom.

Fast forward two years. I was in the front row at a Beach Boys concert in New York City. I couldn't believe it; I was in America, and I was watching my *favorite* band in concert. The band played all their hits to a full crowd in the iconic Central Park, everything from "God Only Knows" to "Good Vibrations" to "Kokomo." Suddenly, lead singer Mike Love brought the show to a halt and pointed me out in the crowd. He did it because he wanted to thank me—he wanted to show his appreciation for the work I had done. Earlier that year, I had produced a film that now opens every Beach Boys concert. The moment he acknowledged me was a surreal moment that I will always treasure.

By that time, I was a very different person. I was no longer being mastered by my vices. I had been clean and sober of drugs and alcohol for over two years. I was now health-conscious, and for the first time in my life, I was working out and being mindful of what I put into my body. I had also managed to quit smoking cigarettes, a habit I'd had for almost a decade.

But it didn't stop there—I also became an avid reader and read over five hundred books, mainly on psychology. I learned meditation and became a daily practitioner. I studied just about every philosophy and strategy on how to increase the quality of the human experience. As a result, I've never had any reoccurring mental health issues—but what's even more remarkable is I truly feel *limitless*. There is nothing I can't accomplish if I set my mind to it. Have I figured everything out? No. In fact, I'll always consider myself a student. But what I have made is *progress*. Progress that has way exceeded my expectations.

I didn't set out to write a book. What you hold in your hands wasn't written as much as it was compiled. Everything I've learned, experienced, and discovered, I've journaled. And as I was going over my notes that I'd written for the last seven years, I had a thought: *"This could be a very helpful book, especially for someone in need of some direction, just like I needed."*

I wrote this book because I want you to know that no matter what your circumstances may be, you can turn things around. If you're reading this, you're blessed; *you're blessed* with the privilege of being alive. It doesn't matter how old you are—you're alive, and anything is possible. In the blink of an eye, life will be over. The last thing you want is to look back and say, "I wish I did more." Take advantage of your most valuable asset: your time on Earth.

I know you don't want to settle for less. I know you want more. I won't promise you the world with this little book, but I do promise that if you participate full out, you will gain clarity of who you are and what you're truly after, and, most importantly, you will increase the quality of your life and the lives of those around you. That's a promise.

I've always believed it's not about the assets you acquire; it's about who you become. That's what will truly fulfill you. It's time to become the person you've always wanted to be. It's time to start living the life you've always dreamed of. It's time to take action. It's time to grow. It's time to give back. It's time to *make history!*

Introduction

Imagine: the human race goes extinct, and all the progress we have made—our history, our evolution, our technology, every book ever written, and everything ever discovered—is completely gone.

Then, after some time, life starts again.

What will come back and what won't?

If you think about it, all our beliefs, thoughts, and languages would be completely different. The reason I point this out is to express to you that life is not as concrete as it may seem. After all, the human race is roughly only 200,000 years old on a planet that's over 4.5 billion years old. We're newcomers; we're still learning. There are a lot of fallacies that most of us take as fact simply because it's part of the human lexicon. But we must remember, nothing on this planet has any meaning except the meaning we give it. Life is what you make of it. You can be whomever you choose to be.

Before we begin, I want to put you into a state of newness. I want you to be as fresh-minded as you were on your first day of school. Right now, I want you to imagine yourself on your first day of school. What were you like? What did you want to be? Did you miss your parents, or were you happy to get away from them?

Let's go back to that fresh mindset, the kind in which you dreamed big. To a time when your beliefs weren't shaped by disappointments, and your personality wasn't modified by the fear of judgment. When you were a kid, the world was magical, and the possibilities were endless. Let's go back there and start a new journey together.

> *"Can you remember who you were, before the world told you who you should be?"*
> — *Charles Bukowski*

This book is not about "positive thinking" or "motivation." This book is about getting clarity about what you want and providing you with the tools and strategies to get it. We'll cover the pivotal steps for achievement, but the truth is— achievement means absolutely nothing if you're not happy and fulfilled. Most achievers only allow themselves to experience happiness when they achieve their goals, but *why would you want to postpone your happiness?* Therefore, this book will also cover the steps you need to strengthen your psychological strength and your emotional fitness, thus allowing you to happily achieve. That way, you can enjoy the journey. And I can tell you from experience: *if you don't enjoy the journey, you probably won't enjoy the destination.*

If you're reading this, you've probably read plenty of other books on growth and development, which is a great habit to have. However, if you're not applying what you learn, then it's futile. We are programmed to think that reading is productive, but that's not always the case. Reading is only a small part of the process. What's most important is applying what you learn—it's about taking action and making progress. And that's what I want for you. After all, **knowing what to do is useless if you don't do what you know.**

Chapter 1:

Beginnings

What's life about for you?

What are you really after?

Neurologically, the only things we want are oxytocin, endorphins, dopamine, and serotonin. These are also known as the "happy brain" chemicals. We're not after the activities on our bucket lists. In actuality, we're after the *feelings* we've associated with these activities. **The reason behind everything we do is to change the way we feel.**

Therefore, goals are not the goal—but feelings are also not the goal, although they are very important. What truly matters with every endeavor is not the achievement, accolade, or affluence; the true prize of any goal is what it makes of you as a person. *It's not about what you get. It's about who you become.*

To truly revolutionize your life and attain fulfillment, you must be *committed* to life mastery. There are areas in life that can't be dabbled with. Health, wealth, relationships, career, psychological strength, and so on—most people only master one of these and dabble in the rest—and they wonder why they're unhappy.

If you want an extraordinary life, you must commit to mastery in all the areas of life that matter. That way, you'll not only have an extraordinary life, but you'll be able to enhance the lives of those around you. Because to truly have a fulfilling life, it can't be just about yourself; it has to be beyond you. *Nothing is going to fulfill you more than being of true value to others.* However, you can't pour from an empty cup.

Look at it this way: when we're given safety instructions at the start of a flight, the instruction is, "In the event of loss of cabin pressure, attend to your own oxygen mask *before* helping anyone else with theirs." For any parent, the natural instinct would be to secure their child's mask before their own, but if they did, they might be unable to help themselves or anyone else. Therefore, to truly be there for others, you must take care of yourself.

> *"The best thing we can do for our relationship with others is to render a relationship to ourselves more conscious. This is not a narcissistic activity. In fact, it will prove to be the most loving thing we can do for the other. The greatest gift to others is our own best self."*
>
> *– James Hollis*

We See Things as We Are

It's much easier to focus on what's wrong with the world than it is to focus on what's wrong with us. We tend to seek things out to criticize because it distracts us from what we really need to work on: *ourselves*.

The truth is, a fulfilled person doesn't squander time on hate. Think about it—if someone is truly happy, why would they waste their time hating?

There are people who vehemently pontificate about how things should be done, yet their own lives could be a complete mess. There's no need to embark on a mission to change the world when there are plenty of changes that could be made in our own lives first. Leo Tolstoy may have said it best: "Everyone thinks of changing the world, but no one thinks of changing himself."

Ironically, our outlook on the world reflects ourselves. As Anaïs Nin famously said, "We don't see things as they are; we see them as we are." If you feel the world is amazing and full of possibilities, you probably view yourself in a similar way. If you feel that most people are rude and deceitful, it's time to question why you feel that way.

> *"Everything that irritates us about others can lead us to an understanding of ourselves."*
>
> *– Carl Jung*

Change begins with the individual, so be the person you want to meet. Proselytizing about how things should be done is not nearly as effective as living it by example. Hating, judging, and complaining won't help you grow. Instead, you can harness that energy and channel it into something constructive.

To help with this, I have come up with a technique: ROF, which stands for Redirecting Our Focus, and you can use it the next time you catch yourself in an unresourceful state.

As soon as you become aware that you're either hating, judging, complaining, or anything similar, start thinking of one of your goals with complete *focus*. If the situation permits it, take some form of action that would bring you closer to that goal, no matter how big or small that action may be.

Another option would be to focus on something you're grateful for. The great thing about gratitude is *you can't be hateful and grateful simultaneously; you also can't be fearful and grateful simultaneously.* So if you find yourself in an unresourceful state, focus on something you're grateful for, and it will put you in a resourceful state. ROF is a great tool for turning something that usually makes us upset into something beneficial. All we have to do is change our focus. Done enough times, it becomes habitual.

An Extraordinary Life

Everyone has the potential to have an extraordinary life, regardless of their age, gender, race, economic status, and so on. For some people this kind of thinking is Pollyannaish, and that's because we've been conditioned to believe that an extraordinary life is an outer game, not an inner game. In actuality, it's a combination of the two, and this is what you need to be most cognizant of—if you want to be fulfilled.

To create an extraordinary life, it is also imperative that you identify what that means to you. By the end of this book, you will most definitely have a clearer vision of the life *you* want and the reasons behind it. It won't be an easy one to achieve, but it will be the one that fulfills you.

Key Points

- The reason behind everything we do is to change the way we feel.

- The true prize of any endeavor is what it makes of you as a person.

- Nothing is going to fulfill you more than being of true value to others.

- To truly revolutionize your life, you must commit to life mastery. Identify the key areas of life that matter to you and master them.

- How we view the world is how we view ourselves. We don't see things as they are; we see them as we are.

- Use the ROF method when you're in an unresourceful state by focusing either on a goal or on something you're grateful for.

Chapter 2:

The Two Worlds

There is something you *must* know, something most people are unfortunately unaware of. It's the reason why we've seen countless people achieve everything they want, yet end up either emotionally broken, chemically addicted, or, in some cases, committing suicide.

We've all heard the stories of people like Michael Jackson, Marilyn Monroe, Anthony Bourdain, Elvis Presley, and countless more. People who were loved worldwide and seemed to have everything a person could want, yet they weren't happy. Why does this happen so often?

Here's the secret: *there are two worlds.* We have the outer world, which entails our career, possessions, achievements (essentially, everything that's external). This is where most people have their focus and where most people think their happiness and fulfillment will come from.

However, there is another world, one that, if neglected, will leave you emotionally broken, and that's the inner world, which is our psychology, emotions, and spirit. It doesn't matter how much you master the outer world; if you neglect the inner world, you'll never be fulfilled.

Remember: what we're chasing with all our endeavors is a *feeling*. But what most people fail to realize is **every desired feeling is already within us and available at any moment.** You don't need to achieve something to feel good.

In the following chapters, there are exercises that will make you uncover your wants. When doing these exercises, be mindful as to which world you're strengthening. It is imperative that you have goals that enhance both worlds. As you now know, achievement means absolutely nothing if you're not fulfilled.

If you take only one thing away from this book, let it be this: **to have an extraordinary life, one in which you're happy and fulfilled, you must master both the inner and outer worlds.**

Key Points

- We have two worlds, the outer world and the inner world.

- The outer world is our career, possessions, achievements—essentially, everything that's external.

- The inner world is our psychology, emotions, and spirit.

- It doesn't matter how much you master the outer world; if you neglect the inner world, you'll never be fulfilled.

- All of us are chasing a feeling. But what most fail to realize is every desired feeling is already within us and available at any moment.

- To have an extraordinary life, one in which you're happy and fulfilled, you must master both the inner and outer world.

READ THIS: I am aware that this is an extremely short chapter and having Key Points for it may seem superfluous. But I'm a firm believer that *repetition is the mother of skill.*

Chapter 3:

Passion

How does one find their passion? For most, the answer is not straightforward. Fortunately, there are strategies that help—tools that can get us moving. The best starting point by far would be to identify your role models. People who fascinate and inspire you. People who've already gotten the results you want. You can learn everything you need to know by studying what they did.

Who Are Your Heroes?
Steve Jobs once said, "One way to remember who you are is to remember who your heroes are," so let's identify yours. Think of the people you respect, be it key figures in history, artists, scientists, or someone you know personally. Who are your heroes?

Your first exercise is to make a list of the people who *truly* fascinate and inspire you. If you have troubling naming ten people, name at least four.

My Heroes

- _____
- _____
- _____
- _____
- _____
- _____
- _____
- _____
- _____
- _____

Once completed, the next step is to figure out *why* you've named these people. What's the commonality among all of them? Is it talent? Is it fame? Is it their lifestyle? Is it their values? Is it their emotional fitness? Is it their economics? Is it their work ethic? List the commonalities of the people you've included.

The Commonalities Among My Heroes

- _____
- _____

- _____

- _____

- _____

- _____

- _____

- _____

- _____

- _____

Once you're done, review what you've written—because you've just written what you want. Although it may not be precise just yet, you now have the broad strokes of what you desire. But it's not enough to know *what* you want; you must identify *why* you want it. Purpose is stronger than outcome.

> *"He who has a why to live can bear almost any how."*
> *– Friedrich Nietzsche*

Look at your answers and ask yourself, "If I had all these things, what would that allow me to feel?" List all the feelings you would experience if you had what your heroes have.

The Resulting Feelings

- _____

- _____

- _____
- _____
- _____
- _____
- _____
- _____
- _____
- _____

By reading over all three lists, you'll have an idea of the type of person you want to become, what you desire, and what feelings you're after.

The reason I asked you to list feelings is because so many of us only allow ourselves to experience happiness or joy when we've done something. We're conditioned to believe that we need a reason to feel good, but that's just not true. Again, _all the feelings you desire are already within you and available at any moment. And the more you access and tap into those feelings, the more resourceful you are to accomplish what you want._

We chase things we had in the past, and now we want more. But usually, we chase things that are scarce, things we were deprived of when we were younger. For example, if someone felt insignificant in high school, they may end up spending the rest of their life chasing significance. Once they get it, they might realize that what they really wanted was love, not significance. I'm not insinuating that it's wrong to want to be significant. My point is to be fully aware of what you're really after and why.

"There is perhaps nothing worse than reaching the top of the ladder and discovering that you're on the wrong wall."
— Joseph Campbell

You may find yourself asking: "How do I know if I'm chasing the wrong thing?" Well, if your goals are all about you feeling significant and being superior to others—and they mainly only benefit you—you're in for trouble. In fact, **selfishness is the root of all suffering.** I'm not saying you won't be able to master the outer world being selfish; it is most definitely possible. However, selfishness ruins the inner world—it will keep you from being fulfilled.

You know you're headed in the right direction if you're operating on love, to grow, or to give back to humanity. Intention is everything, motive does matter. So when you start researching your heroes, make sure you elicit strategies that allow you to experience love and growth—and if you do, you'll be able to provide value to others, which will ultimately fulfill you the most.

If you study any of the greats throughout history, you'll find a common thread: all of them had role models. Legends are a combination of the people they look up to. In fact, just looking at the people you've listed will give you a small preview of what could lie in your future.

Your heroes will play a significant part in your life. I hope you've chosen wisely. Study them. Know their history.

Know the steps they took. You can do this by watching interviews, documentaries, and biopics. You can also read books about them. If they're someone you know personally, you can interview them and elicit their strategies firsthand. In doing so, you'll get a blueprint of what you need to do to become successful yourself.

> *"Study the greats and become greater."*
> *– Michael Jackson*

The research will be enthralling. However, don't use it as a buffer. As soon as you learn something, you must apply it before moving on to something else. Otherwise, it's not research—it's procrastination masked as productivity.

You must also remember to *only take on the skills that are useful.* No one is perfect. Your heroes will have plenty of flaws. When we respect someone or even when we love someone, our vision of them can get impaired—we'll even figure out a way to justify their bad behaviors. You must calibrate and choose which traits to follow and which to ignore. No one is a complete saint, and no one is completely evil, but everyone can teach you something.

It was D.T. Suzuki who said, **"To point at the moon, a finger is needed, but woe to those who take the finger for the moon."** Heroes are here to show you what's possible, to point to the beauty of life and the power of the human spirit. But don't get overly attached and miss the message. Don't put them on a pedestal and idolize. Just respect, appreciate, and learn.

What Are You Already Good At?

What's something people always ask you for help with? Everyone has something they're better at than others. Perhaps the thing you're already good at could be turned into a profession. I know it seems simplistic, but most of us overlook these things. Unfortunately, tons of people are skilled at their hobbies, yet they have a job they hate.

Alternatively, you can think back to when you were in school. What was something you did that no one asked you to do? It wasn't a school project, and your parents didn't tell you to do it, but you did it because you really enjoyed it. Whatever that activity may have been, there is a good chance it could be your passion.

Another option would be to identify an activity that really engrosses you, one that can make hours go by without you even realizing it. When does time fly by for you? For example, if you find that time flies when you're at the gym, you may want to consider pursuing a career in fitness.

Lastly, what's something you can talk about for hours? Whatever that may be, it's certainly worth reviewing—because there's a considerable chance that it's your passion.

The Five Questions

1. If you never had to worry about money, what would you do with your time?

Spend some time with this question. You might be thinking you would just retire and go on an endless vacation, but the truth is, if our entire life was a vacation, we'd get bored.

Vacations don't fulfill us, and that's because we don't grow or make as much progress on vacation.

If money wasn't a limitation, what would you want to achieve in the next ten years? What projects would you take on? Where would you go? What would you do? List your answers.

- _____
- _____
- _____
- _____
- _____
- _____
- _____
- _____
- _____
- _____
- _____
- _____
- _____
- _____
- _____

2. If you could have one wish, what would you wish for?
Rules:
1. You can't wish for more wishes.
2. It can't be anything altruistic.
3. It must be something that's just for you.

_____

_____

_____

_____

_____

_____

3. If there was absolutely no possibility of failure, what would you do?

- _____

- _____

- _____

- _____

- _____

- _____

- _____

- _____
- _____
- _____
- _____
- _____
- _____
- _____

4. *Imagine it's thirty years from now.* TIME Magazine *has listed you as one of the most influential figures of the 21st century. List all the reasons why they picked you.*

- _____
- _____
- _____
- _____
- _____
- _____
- _____
- _____
- _____
- _____

- _____
- _____
- _____
- _____
- _____

5. Imagine the greatest version of yourself—physically, psychologically, financially, and so on. List all the attributes of what you imagine the greatest version of yourself to be.

- _____
- _____
- _____
- _____
- _____
- _____
- _____
- _____
- _____
- _____
- _____
- _____

- _____

- _____

- _____

As I've said before, it's not enough to know what you want. You must also know why you want it. Is it for significance? Is it for love? A lot of people chase their dreams with the hope that it will solve something deeper. Don't make that mistake. Don't just focus on the *activity*—know the *result* you're after.

> *"I think all my success and fame, I have wanted it because I wanted to be loved. That's all. That's the real truth. I wanted people to love me, truly love me. Because I never really felt loved."*
>
> – *Michael Jackson*

The five questions will give you clarity over what your wants are, but *you* must figure out the why. In Michael Jackson's case, he wanted to be the biggest star in the world, and he accomplished it—but he wasn't happy. Because it wasn't the gold records, the sea of fans, or the notoriety that he desired most. What he truly wanted on a deeper level was to be loved. I think we've all been guilty of this in some form; it's so easy to get caught up. But once you identify the actual outcome you want, you might not even have to do the activity you're currently focused on. There might be a better way to get what you want.

Identify What You Don't Want

I'm aware that some of you might find it hard to complete the exercises in this chapter. Perhaps you couldn't identify enough heroes. You can't imagine what you would do if you had all that money or if you were given a wish. Don't worry. If you're not certain about what you want, let's identify what you *don't* want.

Even if you do know what you want, you should still do this exercise, as it will sharpen your vision even more.

Basically, I want you to list everything you don't want: the types of projects you *never* want to work on, the experiences you *never* want to go through, and the environments you *never* want to work in. In other words, I want you to list the qualities of *the career from hell*.

The Career From Hell

- _____

- _____

- _____

- _____

- _____

- _____

- _____

- _____

- _____

- _____

- _____

Once you're done, look at all the things you've listed. The opposite of what you've written is the seed of what you want. As simplistic as this seems, it works. This exercise works for a whole heap of things, not just for identifying your passion. If you're not certain about what you want, identify what you don't want—and that will lead you to what you truly desire.

What's Stopping You?

Perhaps you already know what you want. You know the skills you need to acquire. You know the steps you need to take. Yet you feel there's something that's still in the way.

What is it that holds us back?

The answer is FEAR.

Fear of failure. Fear of being judged. Fear of rejection. All of us deal with fear. The solution is not to get rid of it, because we can't. The solution is to break through fear and not let it control us.

One way to get over a fear is to identify an even bigger fear. For example, if you fear starting a business, focus on the agony, bitterness, and disappointment that would fill you in the future if you don't follow your dreams. Make the fear of not taking action even more scary and painful than the fear of starting. And make the reward for any step toward your dream satisfying. That way, you'll link pleasure to taking action, and link pain to not taking action. Unfortunately, most people have it the other way around.

You'll always have fear in your life. It's part of being human. You just need to learn to use it so it serves you, instead of allowing it to stop you.

Remember This

Ultimately, you must know: *your passion doesn't have to be just one thing.* You don't have to pigeonhole yourself. Take Arnold Schwarzenegger, for example. He demonstrates passion for fitness, filmmaking, and politics. Or Steve Jobs, who merged two of his passions: design and technology.

Often, people paralyze themselves by searching for their one passion, or their one life's purpose. Who says you only have one passion? And who says your passion will be the same ten years from now? It's something that can evolve and branch out. You don't have to have it all figured out. Instead of trying hard to identify the ultimate passion, do what's in front of you with passion.

Key Points

- Identify your heroes and model their strategy for success.

- If your goals are all about you being superior to others, and they mainly only benefit you, you're in for trouble. Selfishness is the root of all suffering.

- You know you're headed in the right direction if you're operating on love, to grow, or to give back to humanity.

- Study how you've answered the five questions—they hold what you desire.

- If you're not certain about what you want, identify what you *don't* want.

- Your passion doesn't have to be just one thing.

- Instead of trying hard to identify the ultimate passion, do what's in front of you with passion.

Chapter 4:

The Power of Guides

You could be the world's most introverted person, but you can't avoid being influenced. I would go as far as saying there is no such thing as an individual. We are all deeply influenced by each other. The great thing is once we become cognizant of this, we can then control what influences us—and decide whose strategies we choose to adopt or drop.

We are *heavily* influenced by what's around us. For instance, if you moved into a house where all your housemates were athletes, you'd be more inclined to exercise. But by that same principle, if you moved into a house where all your housemates were obese, you'd likely develop similar eating habits to them.

Even the music you listen to can have a major influence. For example, people who are rabid fans of rap or heavy metal tend to dress to match the style of music they listen to. It can influence the type of friends they have, the places they go, and, in some cases, it can influence their outlook on life.

It's imperative to be conscious of what influences you. You are what you consume. But as I've said, we do have control. This is where the power of guides comes into play.

"Creativity is the art of concealing your sources."
— *Coco Chanel*

The Beatles were guided into making their seminal album *Sgt. Pepper's Lonely Hearts Club Band* because they were inspired by The Beach Boys' *Pet Sounds*. Michael Jackson didn't invent all the iconic dance moves he's known for. He didn't invent the moonwalk, nor did he invent the "anti-gravity lean." He had many influences that shaped his repertoire. It wasn't Apple or Microsoft that came up with a graphic user interface or the computer mouse—both ideas came from a company called Xerox.

"We have always been shameless about stealing great ideas."
— *Steve Jobs*

Some people are hesitant to have a guide or role model. They insist on being completely original. To them, I say, "Good luck." *Everyone* draws from inspiration. Whether you're aware of it or not, your thoughts, actions, and behavior have been influenced. Of course, this doesn't mean you shouldn't strive for originality, but you should go about it pragmatically.

Create a Guide Folder
Start by creating a Guide Folder. Essentially, compile images of all the things you want, the type of person you want to

become, the places you want to go, the things you want to own, your career goals, your philanthropic goals, and so on. The reason is so you can mentally visualize what an extraordinary life would look like for you—because you need a compelling future, one that genuinely excites you. One reason most people don't take action is because their goals aren't exciting. It's not that they're lazy—it's just that they don't have a compelling future to pull them.

> *"Dream no small dreams, for they have no power to move the hearts of men."*
> *– Johann Wolfgang von Goethe*

Being able to visualize what you want will aid in bringing it into your life. So collect images of everything you want and put them in your Guide Folder, and in doing so, you'll program your brain to focus on the things that matter. Once your brain knows that something is important, you'll naturally see it more often—therefore bringing you closer to the things you want. I know this may sound "airy-fairy," but there's a science to it. There's a network of neurons in your brain called the reticular activating system (RAS for short) which works like a filter. Your RAS decides what to pay attention to. It's why you can tune out a crowd full of people and snap to attention when someone says your name. It's also why when you buy a new car, suddenly you see the same model everywhere you look. By creating a Guide Folder, you will wire your RAS to constantly be on the lookout for the things that matter.

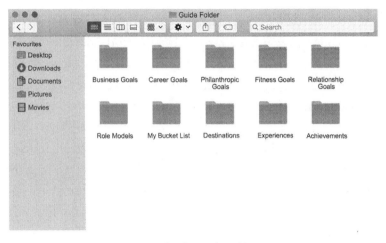

Example of a Guide Folder

Keep the photos in an easily accessible folder on your computer or phone, and look at them often. Each goal should have its own subfolder. As a result, when you go out into the world and see something that's also in your Guide Folder, you will naturally be drawn to it. Perhaps it may lead to something that brings you closer to that goal. At the very least, it will serve as a reminder of what you're after.

> "The only thing worse than being blind is having sight but no vision."
>
> – Helen Keller

One of the many benefits of having a Guide Folder is that you can measure your focus. Once your subfolders become more and more substantial, you'll be able to discern which folder has the most pictures, thus knowing which goal you currently desire most.

How to Create

Have you ever wondered how a movie is made? How a song is composed? Or how a book is written? Especially when it's so remarkable, you can't fathom how one person came up with it? If you do the research, you'll find that creators *always* draw from inspiration.

I'm a fan of Thomas Edison, The Beatles, Michael Jackson, Steve Jobs, and many other luminaries. I have extensively studied the people I respect. What I've found from my years of research is that all of them started as a combination of the people they look up to. Eventually, through years of hard work, they became guides themselves. In the case of The Beatles, they started off as a cover band.

"Most great leaders began in the capacity of followers. They became great leaders because they were intelligent followers."

– Napoleon Hill

For example, if you want to become an artist, start by compiling the works of your favorite artists. Study them—and *ideas will come.*

If you want to write songs, one way of doing it is by making a playlist of the types of songs you aspire to write. Learn the chords, rearrange the order, change the tempo, and you will have something to get you started. Don't just wait around for an idea—draw from what's already out there and build momentum. You don't have to reinvent the wheel. You just need to start.

"I steal from every single movie ever made."
                                    – Quentin Tarantino

This is true for anything, from movies to technology. *Whatever you want to create—compile.* And then study what you compile, find out where the original creator got the idea from, find out what steps the original creator took—and use all of it as a blueprint.

Before moving on to the next chapter, it is *mandatory* that you start your Guide Folder.

"When I want to discover something, I begin by reading up everything that has been done along that line in the past—that's what all these books in the library are for. I see what has been accomplished at great labor and expense in the past. I gather the data of many thousands of experiments as a starting point, and then I make a thousand more."

                                    – Thomas Edison

Key Points

- Be conscious of what influences you—you are what you consume.

- Create a Guide Folder filled with pictures of all the things you want, so you'll have an exciting vision that pulls you.

- One reason why most people don't take action is because their goals aren't exciting. It's not that they're lazy—it's just that they don't have a compelling future.

- Train your brain to always be on the lookout for the things that matter.

- You can create *anything* by drawing from inspiration.

Chapter 5:

Your Manifesto

Now that we've established what an extraordinary life looks like for you by creating a Guide Folder, you now need to craft a story to tie everything together. This is where your manifesto comes in.

Simply put, a manifesto is a mission statement detailing what you want to acquire and accomplish in this lifetime. In this chapter, I'm going to be directing you on how to do just that.

Writing your manifesto will be an integral part of your life. It's something you'll want to spend time on and refine. However, there is space allocated in this book for your first draft. Just listen to your intuition and let it all out. You can fine-tune it later. You don't have to get very specific for now; just the broad strokes will do.

Basically, I want you to write your life story—*the one you want*. This is something I learned from researching Michael Jackson. It was 1979, and Michael was twenty-one. Although he was at an age when most people are still "finding themselves," he managed to write exactly what he wanted. You can use this as an example:

> *"MJ will be my new name. No more Michael Jackson. I want a whole new character, a whole new look. I should be a totally different person. People should never think of me as the kid who sang 'ABC' [or] 'I Want You Back.' I should be a new, incredible actor/singer/dancer that will shock the world. I will do no interviews. I will be magic. I will be a perfectionist, a researcher, a trainer, a master. I will be better than every great actor roped in one. I must have the most incredible training system to dig, and dig, and dig until I find. I will study and look back on the whole world of entertainment and perfect it. Take it steps further from where the greatest left off."*
>
> *– Michael Jackson*
> *November 6, 1979*

Every time I read this, I'm in awe. The fact that he wrote what he was going to do, and did exactly what he set out to do, amazes me. It's easy to look at someone like Michael Jackson and say, "He was born that way." But I don't necessarily look at it like that. He worked hard for it. He didn't predict his future—he made it happen. Michael was someone who had a compelling future, and that's what you need.

Before you get started, let me remind you of something. As we discussed in Chapter 2, *there are two worlds*: the inner world and the outer world. Unfortunately, most people only focus on the outer world. Therefore, most people only have goals for the outer world (Michael Jackson sadly fell into this group). But as you now know, if you don't master your inner world, no amount of money or achievements will ever make you happy.

Here's a suggestion: *have goals for your inner world.* For example, to be psychologically strong and emotionally fit. Or something as simple as the ability to find joy daily. Remember, **the quality of your life is the quality of your emotions.** It doesn't matter how much material wealth you acquire; if you don't master your inner world, you're broke.

Based on what we've gone through, I'm sure you'll have enough career goals—but be sure not to leave out the other vital areas of life such as your health, relationships, and, most importantly, your inner world.

So, let's get started. I want you to write down everything you want in the form of a short essay. Don't worry if your goals seem hard to achieve. The first step is deciding what you want. You can figure out the *how* as you go along.

If you have trouble writing it as an essay, just write a short paragraph and bullet-point the rest. Also, if you lack ideas, refer back to how you answered the five questions in Chapter 3, and to your Guide Folder. Your manifesto should be aligned with both. For this, I want you to be a kid again and dream big. *Pour your heart out.*

_____

_____

_____

_____

_____

_____

_____

_____

_____

_____

_____

_____

_____

_____

_____

_____

_____

_____

_____

_____

Once you're done, your mind will have a narrative of the life you want. Although it's not reality just yet, the story now lives in your mind. It now has a life of its own, stored in the same place where your knowledge and memories reside.

As time passes, you may want to update what you've written, especially once you've accomplished parts of it or perhaps because you've lost interest in some of it. Don't worry about that because right now, your focus should be on getting started and creating momentum; you can course-correct if needed as you go along.

Once you're done with the final draft, it is imperative that you read your manifesto with conviction, so the story becomes more and more real each time. Think of the stories your parents told you when you were a kid. Most of them were fictional, but because you used your imagination, they came to life. I'm sure those stories still live with you today.

Stories can make us laugh, cry, and learn. Stories can affect our biochemistry and physiology. Most importantly, **the story we tell ourselves about who we are, makes us who we are.**

The reason behind writing a manifesto is to ensure that we focus on the things that matter, and to prevent us from getting caught up and losing our way (which happens when we lose our focus). Remember, what you focus on most, you'll experience.

Key Points

- Write your manifesto.

- Be completely honest with what you want.

- Do not neglect your inner world.

- If you lack ideas, refer back to how you answered the five questions in Chapter 3, and to your Guide Folder. Your manifesto should be aligned with both.

- The story we tell ourselves about who we are, makes us who we are.

- What you focus on most, you'll experience.

WARNING

BEFORE MOVING ON TO THE NEXT
SECTION, YOU'LL NEED TO HAVE YOUR
GUIDE FOLDER STARTED, AND YOUR MANI-
FESTO COMPLETED. THIS IS MANDATORY.
WITHOUT DOING SO, YOU WILL NOT GET
THE RESULTS THIS BOOK CAN OFFER YOU.

"If you let your learning lead to knowledge, you become a fool. If you let your learning lead to action, you become wealthy."

— Jim Rohn

Chapter 6:

Inner World Mastery

So far, we've focused mostly on achievements—in other words, the outer world. But now it's time for something deeper. In this chapter, we'll be going over some of the fundamental tools and strategies you'll need to master your inner world.

Most people live at the mercy of what happens in the outer world. They allow it to become the determining factor in how they feel. But you must know that regardless of what happens in the unpredictable outer world, it does not dictate the quality of your life; the quality of your life is the quality of your emotions. I'm here to remind you that regardless of what life throws at you, nothing can take your happiness away. It all starts with making the decision to master your inner world.

"Heaven on Earth is a choice you must make, not a place you must find."

— *Wayne Dyer*

Guard the Mind

An integral part of mastering your inner world is cultivating an astute awareness of what you allow to go on in your mind. The information you feed your mind, the way you talk to yourself, the things you focus on and visualize regularly—all of which dictate the quality of your inner world.

A large part of what plays in our minds is what's wrong or what's missing. It's a survival instinct. The mind is not out to make you happy, and it's also not out to help you achieve—it's focused on avoiding pain and surviving. It's your job to redirect it.

Rarely, if ever, does your mind naturally make you feel happy or make you conquer a particular fear. That's something you have to consciously act on and practice.

Ever been in bed, and you know you should get up, but your mind finds an excuse to sleep for five more minutes?

Ever been on a diet, but your mind rationalizes that it's okay to eat junk food?

Ever decide to feel happy, but an inner voice says, "Don't celebrate just yet—something bad is bound to happen"?

The mind will give you a plethora of reasons to be fearful. It will come up with excuses, tell you it can't be done, convince you to start tomorrow instead of today. **DON'T NEGO-TIATE WITH THE MIND—COMMAND.**

You must demand more and more from the mind. Train it like a muscle. As a result, when you demand that it do something, it does it with less and less hesitation each time. Essentially, the goal is to discipline the mind. Some people may have mixed feelings about discipline; perhaps they associate it with a lack of freedom. But the truth is, **discipline is freedom.** To be lazy is to be enslaved.

Apart from disciplining your mind, don't forget to be mindful of what you allow to go on in your mind—monitor the information you feed your mind—monitor the way you talk to yourself—and be aware of the things you focus on and visualize on a regular basis, as they all play a major role in the quality of your inner world.

Master Your Focus

Did you know we all have the ability to change the way we feel at any moment? All we have to do is change what we're focusing on. Because the truth is **how we feel is dependent on what we're focusing on.** That's why when we're eating, we don't want anyone to talk about things that might make us lose our appetite, or why we don't want to think of our family when we're having sex. *Just a slight shift in focus can drastically change the way we feel.*

If you focus on something that excites you, you'll feel it. If you focus on something that upsets you, you'll feel that too. It sounds so simplistic, but it's true. Let's try something. Pay attention to the way you feel when you focus on the following words: toxic, rape, depression, hate, bigotry, torture, racism. How do these words make you feel when you focus on them?

Now pay attention to the way you feel when you focus on these words: brouhaha, dagnabbit, nincompoop, skedaddle, fartlek, tinkle, and hullaballoo. Notice the difference? Why is that? It's because how you feel is dependent on what you're focusing on.

It's not positive thinking; it's science. A shift in your mind causes a shift in your biochemistry and physiology. For example, if you receive a text that a loved one has been in an accident and is being rushed to the hospital, your heart will start racing, your breathing pattern will change, adrenaline will kick in, and cortisol levels will rise—all of which will drastically change the way you feel. Why? Because a shift in your mind causes a shift in your body.

By shifting your focus, you can…

… change your heart rate

… change your breathing pattern

… change your physiology

… and change your biochemistry.

That's the power of focus.

But it's not enough to change your focus *only* when you catch yourself indulging in negativity. If you really want to take charge of your inner world, you must make it *habitual* to focus on the things that empower you. Focus on what you can control as opposed to what you can't control. Focus on what you're grateful for instead of what's missing.

We're all on the same planet. We're all a part of the human race, and even though all of us have more in common than we have differences—our views on the world (and life) can often be polarizing. For some, the world is a sick place. For others, the world is a beautiful place. And the truth is, whether you believe the world is sick or beautiful, you're right. After all, there's enough evidence for both views. The real question is: *which world do you live in?*

Do you tend to focus on what's wrong with the world and end up getting upset? Or do you focus on the beauty of the world, which puts you in a more resourceful state, and therefore more likely to create change?

I'm not suggesting you ignore what's wrong and focus solely on what's right. There are times when it's healthy to focus on what's wrong. However, the purpose of focus is to put you in a resourceful state, so you can handle whatever comes at you in the best way possible. Think about it: if you focus solely on problems, you'll feel horrible, and if you always feel horrible, it's unlikely that you'll take action.

Now that you're aware of the power of focus, I'm sure you'll be more cautious of what you decide to focus on from day to day. Take advantage of this powerful tool, and you'll realize that you have the ability to change the way you feel at any moment.

Meaning is Malleable

Every occurrence in life inevitably gets labeled. We give meaning to *everything* that happens. But what we don't realize is just how inaccurate these labels can be—and more importantly, we don't realize the effect a disempowering meaning can leave on us.

For example, if someone raises their voice at you, and you say to yourself, "I'm being disrespected," instead of "I'm being challenged," you'll feel and react differently. But if you look at both responses, they could be an accurate representation of the same event. However, I'm sure you'd react differently to being challenged than you would if you felt you were being disrespected.

> *"Man is troubled not by events but by the meaning he gives to them."*
>
> *– Epictetus*

You must remember **meaning is malleable.** Nothing on this planet has any meaning except the meaning we give it. For example, if you don't know what your next move is, does that mean you're lost or searching? If you made a mistake, does that mean you're an idiot or a novice? If your heart starts racing before you're about to meet someone, does that mean you're nervous or excited?

I used to say to myself, "I'm so stressed, I have so much work to do," but then I decided to define my work in a more simplistic way. I now say, "I'm typing on a computer," which makes me feel extremely different. It puts me in a more resourceful state; therefore, I'm less likely to procrastinate and I end up getting more work done.

You have the ability to reframe the meaning of *anything* that happens in life, but that does not mean distorting the truth or deluding yourself—it's training your mind to see things for what they are, and not making them seem worse than they are.

Here's a story that demonstrates just how life-altering it can be to reframe a disempowering meaning. It's a story about a young Steve Jobs. As many of us know, Steve was someone who felt he was chosen and special, but where did that belief come from?

When Steve Jobs was about six years old, he shared the fact that he was adopted with a girl in his neighborhood, to which she responded, "So does that mean your real parents didn't want you?" Steve immediately started crying. He then went to his parents and asked them if it was true that he was abandoned. His parents responded by saying, "No, you don't understand. We specifically picked you out," and they kept repeating that to him with conviction. And from that day forward, Steve always felt he was chosen.

Now, which is true: was Steve Jobs abandoned or was he chosen? The answer is *whichever one you choose*. You can't control all the events in life, but you can control what they mean to you. After all, **it's not the events in life that make us suffer; it's the meaning we attach to them that does.** What we feel is not based on reality, but on our interpretation of reality.

So whenever you come up with a meaning, let it be one that empowers you. Remember: you can reframe the meaning of anything that happens in life.

Gratitude

Most of us know being grateful is important, but not everyone realizes just how powerful gratitude is. In actuality, being grateful is one of the greatest forms of joy. It is also the ultimate antidote for suffering.

In its simplest form, gratitude refers to a state of thankfulness. It's a state that can drastically change the way we feel, and the best part is it's so easily achievable. Here's a tip: don't just practice gratitude. *Step into gratitude.* What does that mean? Well, most people passively list a few things they're grateful for, and although that's good to do, you won't get the full rewards that way. Gratitude has the power to drastically improve your inner world, but you don't reap the rewards unless you play full out.

Instead of just saying to yourself, "I'm grateful to be alive" or "I'm grateful for my family," vividly visualize what you're grateful for, feel the emotions, and let those emotions affect your physiology.

Let's give it a try. List ten things you're grateful for. Whether it's a meaningful experience, a goal you've accomplished, a loved one, the country you live in, or something small.

10 Things I'm Grateful For

1. _____

2. _____

3. _____

4. _____

5. _____

6. _____

7. _____

8. _____

9. _____

10. _____

Now, look back at what you listed. As you go through them one by one, *mentally* see what you've listed. *Focus* on the feelings each gives you—and notice how those feelings affect your body language, how they affect the way you breathe—and how they affect your facial expressions. Totally immerse yourself as if you're experiencing each listing right this moment.

You can also ask yourself questions to enhance the experience. For example:

"What's beautiful about this?"

"How different would my life be without this?"

"Does everyone get a chance to experience this?"

If you do this exercise, you'll realize you can drastically change your emotional state and go from suffering to appreciation in an instant.

Remember, the mind is always looking for what's wrong. It's your job to redirect it. It's your job to focus on what you have instead of focusing on what's missing. Make it a *must* to step into gratitude every single day. After all, what you want is a strong inner world, and just like getting in shape, you can't do it by going to the gym just once in a while.

Movement

Now you know the importance of guarding the mind, the power of focus, the fact that meaning is malleable, and the benefits of gratitude—which is plenty for building a strong inner world. However, I must say that even when you put all these tools into practice, if you don't utilize the power of movement, you'll be missing out on a treasure trove.

We can certainly change the way we feel by changing our focus. However, if you want to make a radical difference in the way you feel, make a radical difference in the way you move.

I'm sure you're aware that human beings have a pattern for every emotion. For example, if someone is angry, they'll take on a certain posture, breathing pattern, and tone of voice. And if someone is joyful, they'll have a different set of physiological attributes to match. We all know the way we feel drastically affects the way we move, breathe, speak, and so on. But not everyone knows that the reverse is also true.

> *"Sometimes your joy is the source of your smile, and sometimes your smile is the source of your joy."*
> — *Thich Nhat Hanh*

Regardless of how sad or stressed you feel, **if you change the way you move, you'll change the way you feel.** This is the reason why countless athletes attribute their psychological fitness to their workouts. Or why so many dancers rave about how dancing de-stresses them and improves the way they feel. The reason is because exercise causes a plethora of changes to the body. It pumps blood to the brain, which helps us think more clearly. It changes our heart rate and the way we breathe. It also makes us release chemicals such as serotonin, dopamine, and endorphins, which make a radical difference in the way we feel. There have also been cases in which physical activity was used as a standalone treatment for people with depression and anxiety.

If you're truly committed to mastering your inner world, you must get committed to movement. Whether it's weight training, running, yoga, dancing, or whatever form of movement that works for you. Not only will this increase your energy and vitality, but it will enhance your inner world, which is even more rewarding.

So if you're overwhelmed, angry, or stressed out, does that mean you should work out right then and there to feel better? No. You don't have to take it to the extreme to get the benefits. You could go for a short walk, jog, or even do a few jumping jacks, and you'll feel the difference. I know it may sound silly and simplistic, but it works. Remember: if you change the way you move, you'll change the way you feel.

Commit to Happiness

Ultimately, the goal of mastering the inner world is the attainment of happiness and fulfillment. And like any goal, it requires commitment. All of us desire a fulfilling life, but not everyone is truly *committed*. Happiness is a habit, but it's also a responsibility.

I believe most people have their hearts in the right place, but since most aren't aware of the importance of the inner world, their happiness is always at the mercy of the outer world. And the problem is we can't always control the outer world. Accidents, injustice, natural disasters, and deaths are just some of the things we have no control over.

Some people put tremendous time and effort into making themselves happy. And through all their efforts, they achieve a quality of life that truly fulfills them. Yet when they go through some form of adversity, like someone they love passes away, they forfeit their happiness.

In life, things won't always go your way. You will always have problems. You will always suffer. But you must realize that no matter what life throws at you, nothing has the power to take your happiness away (unless you let it). Of course, this doesn't mean you won't experience agony beyond comprehension from time to time. It's not always possible to avoid sorrow. But if you commit to happiness, you'll find that you can always find your way back to happiness and fulfillment, regardless of what you go through.

After all, there are so many people who've lost limbs, lost families, been through *hell on Earth*, yet they still find a way to be happy. The question is: *are you committed to being happy no matter what life throws at you?*

I plead with you: get committed to mastering your inner world, and you'll attain a level of happiness and fulfillment like you've never imagined. I promise you if you master your inner world, you'll be mentally, emotionally, and spiritually equipped to handle *anything* that comes your way.

Key Points

- The quality of your life is the quality of your emotions.

- The mind is not out to make you happy or help you achieve. It's focused on avoiding pain and surviving. It's your job to redirect it.

- How you feel is dependent on what you're focusing on.

- Meaning is malleable.

- Gratitude is one of the greatest forms of joy and the ultimate antidote for suffering.

- If you change the way you move, you'll change the way you feel.

- Commit to happiness and you'll find that no matter what life throws at you, nothing can take your happiness away.

Chapter 7:

Taming the Ego

It's easy to overlook just how harmful the ego can be. Because it can be a great motivator, but it has its fair share of setbacks: it slows us down and stunts our growth, it does way more harm than good, and, more importantly, it keeps us from being fulfilled. However, the solution is not to kill the ego. In fact, it's impossible to do so. Our goal is to tame it.

Before we get into this, I must make clear what the ego really is—*it's just fear*. It all stems from the universal fear that we're not enough—whether it's not being smart enough, rich enough, young enough, attractive enough, and so on. Ultimately, we believe that if we're not enough, we won't be loved. That's all the ego is. *It's the fear of not being worthy of love.*

The Dangers of the Ego

According to the Oxford Dictionary, "ego" is defined as "a person's sense of self-esteem or self-importance," which doesn't seem bad. It just sounds like having confidence, but don't let that fool you. If you dissect further, you'll find that although an untamed ego may aid in garnering material success, it keeps us from being happy and fulfilled. It doesn't matter how successful you are—if you have an untamed ego, it will always overpower your actions. Your happiness will always be at the mercy of some outside source.

As I've pointed out, we can't kill the ego. The ego rises and subsides, similarly to anger, but we can manage and tame it. Think of the ego like a muscle. The more you use it, the stronger it becomes; the less you use it, the weaker it gets. There is a quote by Native American Sitting Bull that gives great insight: "Inside of me there are two dogs. One is mean and evil, and the other is good. When asked which one wins, I answer, the one I feed the most." This applies to how our ego can be shaped. The more we indulge and invest in egotistical behavior, the stronger it becomes. If we stop feeding it, it weakens.

I have personally seen the adverse effects of an untamed ego firsthand. It's something I learned the hard way, and it took me years to figure out how to manage it. I hope that by reading this, you won't have to go through that long learning curve.

Build Strength by Being the Weakest
One way to tame the ego is to fill your life with people who are doing better than you, be it financially, physically, or career-wise. Not only will this humble you, but it will also push you to work harder.

Look at it this way. If you were to run a race with people who aren't as fast as you, surely you'd win. But if you run with people who are faster than you, you may not win, but *you'll perform better.* Therefore, if you're not the fastest, strongest, or smartest person in the room, don't let it intimidate you; let it inspire you. Revel in the fact that there is so much you can learn from the ones around you.

If you're having trouble finding high achievers to surround yourself with, do so with the content you watch, the books you read, and the people you research. Watching interviews of the people you respect can be more valuable than going to college *if* you implement what you learn and take action.

Ego vs. Confidence

The key message of this chapter is to be conscious of how the ego can hold you back, but it doesn't mean you shouldn't strive to be the best, and it certainly doesn't promote being a pushover. It pays to be assertive, but be mindful as to whether it's ego or confidence. As I've said, ego is fear. Confidence, on the other hand, is a sense of certainty that you're able to perform. Know the difference.

The purpose of this chapter is also to remind all of us to have more humility and to remember that it's more important to grow than to win. Have big dreams, see yourself as victorious, but be humble and have respect for others. The ego can drive you, but you must remember that it will never fulfill you.

Monitor the Ego

Take a moment to reflect. Think of the last time you felt the ego arise. Perhaps you got upset, offended, or triggered. Maybe it led to an argument. Ask yourself: "Did that situation make me feel less worthy of love?"

The truth is the ego only arises when our worth is questioned. As I've said, we all fear that we're not enough—at least in some area of our life—and when that nerve gets hit, the ego arises. Every one of us has an area in our life where we feel inadequate, and that strengthens our fear of not being worthy of love, but we can't let it affect the quality of our lives. Change is a must.

Like most behavioral change, it starts with making the decision to do so. And if you've come this far, I know you'll be doing just that. To complete the process of change, we go through four stages. The following is a glimpse into the process of how we learn:

Stage 1: Unconscious incompetence
You're doing it wrong, but you're unaware.

Stage 2: Conscious incompetence
You're doing it wrong, but you're aware.

Stage 3: Conscious competence
You're doing it right, but it requires effort and thought.

Stage 4: Unconscious competence
You're doing it right, but it happens almost effortlessly.

The four stages of learning can be applied to learn anything, but for the purpose of this chapter, we'll look at how it relates to taming our ego. Before reading this, you were probably at Stage 1. You had an untamed ego, like a lot of us, and you were unaware of it. Now that you're reading this, you're aware—meaning you're now slowly moving on to Stage 2: Conscious incompetence. Stages 3 and 4 will happen when you begin implementing the five habits shared at the end of this chapter.

Generally, when people set goals, it's usually to have a successful business, own a big house, and so on. It's good to have these types of goals, but having goals that enhance your inner world, like taming the ego or achieving emotional fitness, is even more important because it affects the way you feel every single day.

The Ego in Conversations

One of the most adverse effects of having an untamed ego is that it often leads to altercations. As I said before, someone with an untamed ego has a need to project superiority to combat the insecurity of not being enough, which usually leads to altercations. It also prevents them from learning new things.

In conversation, always seek to learn, not to teach. Instead of trying to project superiority, *learn*. Ask yourself:

"In what ways is this person superior to me?"

"What do they know that I don't?"

"What can I learn from them?"

Not only will this help build stronger connections, but you'll also get to learn. However, if you find yourself in disagreement with someone (which will happen), try your best to see it through their eyes. Try to understand and appreciate their world. Even if you still feel the same after looking at it from their perspective, don't argue; let it go. As Dale Carnegie said, "A man convinced against his will is of the same way still."

We might love something that someone else hates but focusing on our differences doesn't help us connect or grow. Instead, find commonality and connect. That way you can learn from one another. Everyone you meet can teach you something. Everyone you meet is superior to you in some way.

> *"When you talk, you are only repeating what you already know. But if you listen, you may learn something new."*
> *– Dalai Lama*

John Ferriter, a friend of mine, in my opinion said it best: **"It's more important to do right than to be right."** This doesn't mean you shouldn't fight for what's right, but if you're arguing for the sake of arguing, it's pointless.

Achieve Social Freedom

As I mentioned earlier, most of the time we don't go after what we want because of fear. The fear of being judged is probably the most prevalent.

The truth is, we all care about what people think of us. We even care about what strangers think of us, which is crazy. I'm sure you've heard that we shouldn't care about what people think of us, but the truth is *you can't stop caring completely*, and thankfully so, because to not care at all about the opinions of others would be tantamount to being a psychopath. The real trick is not to let the opinions of others control you.

One of the most important decisions you must make is that you won't allow yourself to be controlled by the opinion of others. In doing so, you'll achieve social freedom. What is social freedom? Social freedom is having the ability to behave the way you feel is right, without letting the fear of judgment, rejection, or embarrassment modify you. Essentially, it's claiming your sovereignty and not letting the opinions of others control you.

How does one go about achieving social freedom? One way to start is by pushing your social boundaries, whatever those may be for you. *What's something you're not doing because you fear you'd be judged?* Once you've identified that, make the decision to overcome it. Start small and build up.

For example, if you're the type of person who has trouble conversing with strangers, start by smiling at them, then slowly progress to asking them for the time or directions, and build up from there. What's the point of this? It's an exercise to build your social freedom muscles. It's also an exercise to overcome fear. The reason we have social boundaries is because we fear either judgment, rejection, or embarrassment (sometimes it's all three), but we can't let these forces control our life. After all, if you avoid what you fear, you'll also avoid what you desire.

Ultimately, you want to get to a point where you're able to live life on your terms. Social freedom does not mean you stop listening to people. After all, some of our best lessons come from the people around us. The goal is *freedom*. It's not allowing fear to hold you back from being the person you want to be.

Five Habits to Tame the Ego

1. Commit to never-ending improvement

Only a fool knows everything; a wise man knows how little he knows. Remember, everyone you meet can teach you something, and everyone you meet is superior to you in some way. Never stop learning.

2. Don't let the opinions of others control you

Make the decision that you will not allow yourself to be controlled by the opinions of others. Although it's human nature for us to care about what people think of us, we must never allow the opinions of others to *control* us. You can listen to people, but they shouldn't have the power to stop you from being the person you want to be.

3. Let go of the need to always be right

Remember: it's more important to do right than to be right. Some things *are* worth fighting for, especially if it makes a difference. However, if you often find yourself in altercations with people, and the only result is resentment and division, then it's completely pointless and destructive. Focus on what brings us together, not what tears us apart.

4. Remind yourself that it's just fear

When the ego arises, remember it's just fear, the fear of not being worthy of love—which is an illusion.

5. Question the ego

Any time the ego arises, question it. Ask yourself:

"Does this situation make me less worthy of love?"

The answer is a resounding NO. Remember, the ego will only arise when our worth is being questioned. But if you question it back, the fact that it's an illusion becomes apparent, and by doing so, the ego loses its power.

Key Points

- Ego is nothing but the fear of not being worthy of love.

- We all fear that we're not enough—at least in some area of our life—and when that nerve gets hit, the ego arises.

- Having an untamed ego may help you garner material success, but it will keep you from being fulfilled.

- Inner world goals like taming the ego are the most crucial goals because they affect the way you feel every single day.

- It's more important to do right than to be right.

- Commit to never-ending improvement.

Chapter 8:

Dealing With Adversity

In life, events happen that we truly can't control. Someone we love passes away. A natural disaster occurs. Our country goes to war. Regardless of how well we prepare, problems will *always* be around—*but so will solutions.*

There might be something you're going through right now that's causing you a lot of mental anguish. As tough as it can be, you still have a choice: *will you let it paralyze you or will you let it drive you?*

Adversity can be extremely tough to deal with, but it's never *all* bad. It is my core belief that **everything that happens in life benefits us in some way.** I consider the day I hit rock bottom, which was the day I ended up in the psychiatric unit diagnosed with bipolar disorder, to be one of the most valuable experiences I've ever had. Why? Because it gave me the impetus to change. At the time, I considered it "the worst day of my life," but now I look at it as a gift.

> *"Rock bottom became the solid foundation on which I rebuilt my life."*
>
> *– J.K. Rowling*

No matter what you're going through, realize that no problem is permanent. No problem will affect your entire life. And as trite as it may come across, *that which does not kill us makes us stronger*, as said by Friedrich Nietzsche.

Apart from making us stronger, adversity also teaches us valuable lessons that good times never can. We can then either sulk in our pain and give up, or we can use it. For example, we can make it our mission to prevent others from going through what we did. As Oprah Winfrey said, "Turn your wounds into wisdom."

The purpose of this chapter is in no way to downplay adversity or to discount what you may be going through. My intention is to give you the insights that will enable you to access resourceful states so you can handle whatever comes at you in the best way possible. I also want to ensure that you don't waste your pain. After all, pain is the ultimate motivator.

Let Negativity Drive You

Happiness is nothing without sadness. It's our misfortunes that make us value the beauty of life, and it's also our misfortunes that make us grow.

The shift to using negativity to drive you can be boiled down into one sentence: **PAIN IS FUEL.** Study any of the greats throughout history and you will find tremendous adversity in almost every case. **You will never come across a strong person who had an easy past.**

Although this chapter is aimed at helping you handle "negative emotions," the truth is there are no negative emotions. **Every emotion serves us.** Every emotion has its purpose. Just like how everything in life has its purpose.

The moment we recognize the benefits that come from adversity, we can then see adversity for what it truly is: a blessing. No matter what you go through, as long as you take something from the experience, in the end you'll be thankful for all of it. Remember: pain is fuel.

The Comparing Game

A big mistake a lot of us make is we compare ourselves to others. At times it's useful, as it can raise our standards. But done too often, it robs us of our joy and causes us to unnecessarily suffer.

The comparison game can be detrimental because it's never-ending. No matter how far we go in life, there will always be someone who's better than us at something. If you're the richest person on Earth, someone else might have a better relationship. If your body is in perfect shape, someone else might have a better career. Even if you're Elvis Presley, the King of Rock and Roll, or John Lennon, founder of The Beatles, someone else will have a leg up on you. In the case of these two men, they both died in their forties. They didn't get the gift of a full life.

However, we must remember that *pragmatically* comparing ourselves to others does have its merits. But we must never allow it to *hinder* our growth and cause us to suffer. Have an "If they can, so can I" attitude, not a "They're so far ahead, why should I even bother?" attitude. **Trade jealousy for inspiration. Don't get bitter; get better.**

If you constantly compare yourself to others, you'll feel lousy. Life will seem too daunting, and you'll most likely give up. Instead, compare yourself with who you were yesterday. As long as you're making progress, celebrate!

> *"There is nothing noble in being superior to your fellow man; true nobility is being superior to your former self."*
> *– Ernest Hemingway*

Celebrate Progress

The best way to deal with anything that life throws at us is by *making progress*. Achieving our goals or ticking something off our bucket list may excite us for a period of time, but it doesn't last. The only thing that's going to keep us fulfilled for the long term is progress.

> *"If you want to know the secret to happiness, I can give it to you in one word: progress. Progress equals happiness."*
> *– Anthony Robbins*

Progress, no matter how small or slow, should always be celebrated. The reason is to associate pleasure with taking action, so it makes us want to do it more often. It can be something small like losing one pound, which anyone should be proud of accomplishing. Some people tend to feel disappointed for only losing one pound—they'll get upset, they won't reward themselves, and eventually they'll give up. The trick is you must celebrate your progress, no matter how negligible it may seem. This will help you stay on the path.

> *"The more you celebrate your life, the more there is in life to celebrate."*
> — *Oprah Winfrey*

You Will Miss This

Sometimes, we get so caught up in our problems and where we're headed, we forget to appreciate what we have. But you must understand that **no matter how much you want things to change, one day you will miss what you have now.**

You probably have exciting goals that you can't wait to achieve—which is important for all of us to have—but don't forget that once you get there, certain things won't be the same. People in your life now may not be around anymore. Perhaps you lose your parents. Your child grows up and moves to another country. War happens, and your city is never the same. It's important to want change, but we *must* appreciate the journey and enjoy the moments along the way.

Remember, no matter how much you want things to change, one day you will miss what you have now. Today is the "simpler time" you'll reminisce about tomorrow.

Perspective

We live in a world where there are wars, people dying of hunger, natural disasters, and injustices that happen every single day. Historically, we have put people in the most horrid situations, from beheadings to concentration camps. The human race has been through a lot. Yet a lot of us still sweat the small stuff. We forget just how blessed we are. In terms of living standards, we are living in the *greatest time in history*, but we certainly don't always act like it.

If you're reading this, chances are you have resources that billions of people don't. Over three billion people don't have internet access. Over two billion people live on less than $4 a day. Over seven million children die every year from preventable and treatable causes. *We're not in scarcity. We're able to give back.*

However, please understand I am in no way discounting the pain you may be going through. I understand that everyone is on different parts of the journey. Things can be hard. *But we don't have to make it harder than it is.* It's healthy to acknowledge pain and understand the message behind it, but we must never amplify it. We must have the right perspective and use adversity to drive us forward, not hold us back.

> *"I cried because I had no shoes, then I met a man with no feet."*
>
> – *Mahatma Gandhi*

With everything that goes on in life, it's easy for us to forget that **there are people who would love to have our bad days.** Our worst day is someone else's dream. Regardless of what you're going through, if you're reading this, you're able to give back—and in doing so, you can't help but heal yourself in the process.

Key Points

- Everything that happens in life benefits us in some way.

- Happiness is nothing without sadness.

- Every emotion serves us. Every emotion has its purpose.

- Trade jealousy for inspiration. Don't get bitter; get better.

- The only thing that's going to keep us fulfilled for the long term is *progress*.

- No matter how much you want things to change, one day you will miss what you have now.

- There are people who would love to have our bad days.

Chapter 9:

Questions

I've always been curious about what makes us who we are. What determines our likes and dislikes? What shapes our decisions? What dictates our behavior? For years, I looked for an expeditious way to get to the core of the human psyche, and one of the things I found which proved to be the most profound is that each of us has a *blueprint*. Our blueprint determines the way we view and experience the world—it is the software that runs our lives.

Simply put, our blueprint is our beliefs, rules, values—it's our model of the world. Obviously, our blueprint was not something we constructed consciously. Therefore, there are aspects in everyone's blueprint that holds them back. Unfortunately, most people aren't aware that they have a blueprint. So it never gets uncovered, much less updated. You could be running the same software that was wired twenty years ago that's completely not suitable for what you want today.

You can get a sense of your blueprint by examining your fashion sense, the books you read, your role models—but the most practical way is by asking questions. Ask yourself the right questions and you'll get to know your beliefs, your rules, your values, and what you've attached pain or pleasure to—all of which make up your blueprint.

Questions are an incredibly practical tool, though most of us don't realize their true potential. That's why this chapter is focused on questions, but not just any questions—questions that give us purposeful answers. Questions that get to the depth of what's running our life.

Ultimately, the questions included in this chapter are for you to uncover your blueprint so you're familiar with the software that's running your life, and for you to determine whether your current blueprint fits your current goals.

These questions can also be used on your friends, family members, colleagues, and so on. They'll give you a deeper understanding of the people in your life, therefore building stronger connections. Purposeful questions are also massive time-savers; if you asked someone all the questions included and listened intently, you'd get to know things about them that even those closest to them don't.

The Rules
What's most important is not *what* you answer, but *why* you've chosen that answer. For example, when asked, "What's life about for you?" some might say, "Life is about love." Others might say, "Life is about achievement." Your answer will be dictated by your blueprint. The intention is not just to point out what's right or wrong, but for you to familiarize yourself with your blueprint, and once you do, you then need to decide

if your blueprint needs to be updated or not (in most cases, it does).

Asking yourself these questions is straightforward. However, when asking someone else, calibration is needed. First, it's unlikely that someone will be comfortable being asked all these questions in one sitting. That would be too intrusive for most. So ask intelligently. Be mindful of how the questions are being received and calibrate as you go.

Regardless of what a person answers, don't judge. You can't connect with someone when you're judging them. Also, make sure you pay close attention to the answers and build a dialogue. Don't just sit there thinking about the next question. Listen, learn, enjoy, and connect.

The Opening Act

Who are you?

Who are you not?

Who do you *have* to be?

What's your favorite word?

What's your least favorite word?

What's your favorite curse word?

If you were in a room with all the people you've ever met in your life, who would be the first person you'd look for?

What's your favorite quote?

What sound or noise do you love?

What's your favorite scent?

What was your first job?

What's the best job you've ever had?

What's the worst job you've ever had?

Would you rather be a world-class rock star or a world-class athlete?

What turns you on?

What turns you off?

Would you rather have unlimited money or endless love and happiness?

What's a song that you know all the lyrics to?

What's one movie you can watch again and again?

Which fictional world would you most like to visit?

If you could only read one book for the rest of your life, which one would it be?

Who was your childhood celebrity crush?

What's something that makes you smile?

What's something that makes you laugh?

What are you most grateful for?

What's the best vacation you've ever had?

Is the world a friendly place?

Who would you trade places with for a day?

If you could meet any three people, dead or alive, who would you pick?

If you could be best friends with any living person, who would you pick?

Which historical event do you most vividly remember?

If you could travel back in time and witness three historical events, which ones would you choose?

What superpower would you like to have?

If you had to choose to live without one of your five senses, which one would you pick?

If your house was on fire and you could only save one item, what would it be?

What's something most people don't know about you?

What's something you will always say no to?

What's something people should pay more attention to?

What product would you like to see invented?

What's missing on Earth?

What are you addicted to?

If you could create one law that everyone in the world had to follow, what would it be?

What do you think of tattoos? Would you ever get one?

What's your opinion on recreational drugs?

What's on your bucket list?

What did you learn today?

The Main Attraction

What's life about for you?

What's most important to avoid in life?

What's one of the most magnificent moments of your life?

What are you most passionate about?

If you had $10 million to give away to any cause, which cause would you choose?

If you could end world hunger by killing one innocent person, would you?

What's one of your life rules?

What percentage of you do people know? (For example, if the answer is 60%, dissect the other 40%.)

What makes you different from most people?

Are you happier now, or were you happier when you were a kid?

Which parent are you closer with and why?

What do you like about the way you were parented?

What do you dislike about the way you were parented?

What does it mean to be a friend?

What does it mean to be married?

What does it mean to be a parent?

What is love?

What has to happen for you to feel loved?

What does success mean to you?

What has to happen for you to feel successful?

What do you wish you were better at?

What's a reoccurring dream you have?

When was the last time you pushed yourself out of your comfort zone?

When are you happiest?

When are you saddest?

How old do you feel?

What's something someone once said to you that you will never forget?

What's something you did recently that's worth remembering?

What's something you can teach?

What are three skills that everyone should learn?

What are your three highest-value activities?

What's the best investment you've ever made?

What's something you need to fix in your life?

What brings out the best side of you?

What brings out the worst side of you?

What's your biggest failure?

What's your biggest fear?

What's something you're proud of?

What's something you're ashamed of?

What's the best thing you've done?

What's the worst thing you've done?

For an all-expenses-paid vacation to a destination of your choice, would you rip off the wings of a butterfly?

What's the best advice you've ever received?

What's the worst advice you've ever received?

Encore

What's something you long believed to be true and later realized wasn't?

What's something you know is true, but most people don't agree?

What's your most controversial opinion?

What's the biggest thing you've changed your mind about in the past five years?

What's one piece of advice you think would be practical to instill in a newborn baby's mind?

Where do you see yourself in ten years?

Do you believe you have a soul?

Do you believe in God?

If past lives are real, what do you think yours was?

What's the meaning of life?

If you only had five years left to live, what would you do differently?

How do you spend the last hour of your day?

How would you like to spend the last hour of your life?

How would you prefer to die?

How do you wish to be remembered?

Where would you like to go after death?

If you could start life all over again, would you? And what would you do differently?

Imagine you're on your deathbed, surrounded by loved ones; what would your parting words be?

Key Points

- Our blueprint determines the way we view and experience the world. It is the software that runs our lives.

- Our blueprint is not something we constructed consciously. Therefore, it needs to be uncovered and updated.

- Questions are an expeditious way to uncover our blueprint.

- Ask the right questions, and you'll get to know your beliefs, rules, values, and what you've attached pain or pleasure to—all of which make up your blueprint.

- Questions also help us build deeper connections, as they allow us to get to the core of people.

- What's most important is not *what* you answer, but *why* you've chosen that answer. Remember, your answers will be dictated by your blueprint.

Chapter 10:

You Already Know

You may not know it all, but you most definitely know enough to get moving. You may feel uncertain at times, *but so does everyone else.* No one has life all figured out, but that doesn't stop them from having an extraordinary life, and it shouldn't stop you.

You may be asking yourself: "If I knew what to do, then why am I not doing it?" There are several possibilities, but the most likely reason is an ineffective strategy.

You may also be asking: "If it's easy to succeed, why isn't everyone successful?" The reason is because it's *easier* not to be successful, especially in the short term. Watching movies is easier than going to the gym. Keeping the job you hate is easier than pursuing your passion. But remember, **if you only do what's easy, life will be difficult.**

Reflect on this: *everyone* knows how to lose weight, but not everyone is in shape. Everyone knows that to be rich, you need at least some form of financial intelligence, but most people aren't willing to put in the time. It's not that there isn't a solution; it's just that not everyone uses it.

You may be thinking: "This is great, but I just don't have the time, the money, the opportunity—or in other words: the resources." But the truth is resources are never the real problem. The real problem is a lack of resourcefulness.

Trust me; you already know enough to get going. I'll prove it to you. If I were to ask you to list fifteen ways to get financially independent or fifteen ways to achieve any goal you have, undoubtedly you could—and most definitely, one (or more) of the ways you list would work. It's just a matter of *taking action, being persistent, and having a compelling future to pull you through.*

The Fifteen List

For our final exercise, I want you to list two goals you want to achieve in the next six months to a year. Goals that truly excite you. Goals that will take you to the next level. Perhaps they seem impossible, but in your heart you know that if you take action and persist, they're achievable.

After that, I want you to list fifteen different ways you could achieve each goal. List whatever your mind comes up with, no matter how unorthodox it may seem.

Goal 1: _____

Ideas on how to achieve it:

1. _____

2. _____

3. _____

4. _____

5. _____

6. _____

7. _____

8. _____

9. _____

10. _____

11. _____

12. _____

13. _____

14. _____

15. _____

Pick one idea that you will start taking action on today:

_____

Goal 2: _____

Ideas on how to achieve it:

1. _____

2. _____

3. _____

4. _____

5. _____

6. _____

7. _____

8. _____

9. _____

10. _____

11. _____

12. _____

13. _____

14. _____

15. _____

Pick one idea that you will start taking action on today:

_____

Once you're done, you'll need to complete the most crucial step: *setting a deadline*. And for it to be truly effective, you'll also need to come up with a form of punishment, which you'll only implement in the event you don't follow through.

A goal without a deadline (or schedule) is merely a fantasy, and that's why it's crucial for you to have a deadline. However long you give yourself to accomplish a task is how long you'll take. If you have a week to finish a project, it will take a week. If you have three months to finish that same project, it will take three months. Therefore, your last step is to set a deadline and punishment for both goals. Examples of punishments include eating dog food, shaving your head, or even banning yourself from listening to your favorite artist or band for a year. Whatever works best for you. Just make sure it's something that you're willing to do *whatever it takes* to avoid.

I'm aware that this little exercise may seem bizarre to some, but it works. Our survival mind will do anything to avoid pain. So the more painful your punishment, the more likely you are to follow through.

Goal 1
Deadline: _____

Punishment: _____

Goal 2
Deadline: _____

Punishment: _____

Lastly, to truly solidify this, get some accountability. Tell people, especially those you don't want to disappoint. That way, there's no turning back.

Now for the fun part: taking action. If the first idea you try doesn't work, try another idea from your list. Remember, if you fail, you don't have to change your goal. Just change your approach.

Anyway, you know what to do, so what are you waiting for? As I've said before, knowing what to do is useless if you don't do what you know. **Too many people settle for "I know this" as opposed to "I'm doing this."** Take action now.

We all have varying life conditions. Some are dealt a better hand; others are forced to hold their hands out. But you must remember that your background, age, race, gender, or economic status does not determine your future. For it's not our conditions that determine our future; it's our decisions. The decision to take action, grow, give back, and eventually... make history.

Key Points

- You already know enough to get moving.

- Resources are never the real problem. The real problem is a lack of resourcefulness.

- Set two goals to accomplish in the next six months to a year.

- Set non-negotiable deadlines for both goals.

- Set punishments to be implemented if you don't meet your deadlines.

- Have accountability for both goals.

- Too many people settle for "I know this" as opposed to "I'm doing this."

Closing:

Our Three Billion Seconds

At the start of this book, I told you to imagine the human race going extinct—and eventually life starting again. If things go back to square one, *what will come back and what won't?* This is something I think about often. If we get wiped out and after some time life starts again, it would be another species that occupies Earth. However, the question remains: what will come back and what won't? The truth is most of the things we think of from day to day will not return. Why? Because the world is what *we* make of it. **We don't experience reality. We experience our interpretation of reality.**

The purpose of this book is to remind all of us of just how much power and control we have and how our limitations are merely psychological. Don't be bamboozled by social conditioning. Nothing on this planet has any meaning except the meaning we give it. If the meaning you've attached to something is serving you, be conscious of how it does. But if it's limiting you, you have the power to reframe it. *Claim your sovereignty*, and if you do, you'll experience growth way beyond your expectations.

But what's the point of growing? **The reason we grow is so we have more to give.** I promise you, nothing will fulfill you more than being of true value to others. And nothing will depress you more than solely focusing on yourself. Selfishness is the root of all suffering. To step out of it, find a way to serve.

Did you know that one billion seconds is about thirty-one years long? When I found this out, it blew my mind because that means the average lifespan (which is about seventy to eighty years) is *less* than three billion seconds. **Less than three billion seconds is all we get!** Life is a flash; in the blink of an eye, it's all over. As I've said before, the last thing you want is to look back and say, "I wish I did more."

As our journey here comes to an end, I must thank you for your time. We've gone through a lot together; I truly hope that I've served you. Before you go, I'd like to ask you for a favor. Promise me you'll do whatever it takes to attain the quality of life you want. In your heart, you know that if you take action and persist, you will get whatever your heart desires.

Even though our time on Earth is limited, our capabilities aren't. The human race continues to impress and inspire. I often wonder what we as a species will do next. After all, the world has been around for 4.5 billion years, but humans have only been around for 200,000 years.

We've only just begun.

Acknowledgments

In a perfect world, I would be able to show my utmost gratitude daily to each and every one of you who has impacted my life—that's how fortunate I've been. The myriad of wonderful people I've had the honor of spending time with is unfathomable. I want to start by apologizing in case there are any omissions. It's not my intention to exclude anyone.

I am beyond grateful to my loving family: my parents, Umapathy Jaisi and Ganga Daybi, and my wonderful siblings, Kreshenka and Vivandra Jaisi. To Sandra Bai, Sandra Chettri, Harleen Dip Kaur, Dr. Harjit Sidhu, Sanjay Madhav, Suraj Chettri, Asha Devi, and the rest of my beautiful family who has taught me so much, too many to list.

My life has been enriched beyond words by Harbir Gill, Mike and Jacquelyne Love, John Stamos, Bruce Johnston, Jeffrey Foskett, Leif Garret, Michael Lloyd, and Alan Boyd; I don't know where'd I'd be without the kindness and support from each and every one of you.

I also want to thank John Ferriter, Jennifer Safrey, Noor Kay, Dani Komari, Saloua El Babsiri, Ameesha Green, Tommy Organ, Jermaine Jackson, Marlon Jackson, Tito Jackson, Jackie

Jackson, Vic Kettle, Shimy Latif, Rossnan Cheong, Shaza Nikmah, Hubert Chua, Naseem Nelson, Justin Roseworn, Dean Sim, Jordan Sam, Kingsley Warner, Moustapha Koutoub Sano, Lewis Howes, Matthew Cesaratto, and Leo Sayer.

I am where I am today because of a lifetime of kindness from family, friends, mentors, colleagues, kindred spirits, and loyal fans. Many of you had a direct hand in the creation of this book. Hundreds more have made lasting contributions to my life. Each of you deserves to be acknowledged, but the list would never be complete. So I will close by saying thank you for sharing some of your time with me. God bless you all.

– NJ, Kuala Lumpur, 2022

About the Author

Noven Jaisi is an award-winning filmmaker, producer, writer, coach, and philanthropist. His creative abilities have made him one of the most sought-after talents of the 21st century. Noven's mission is to serve humanity by bringing people the tools, strategies, and content that are guaranteed to drastically enhance the human experience.

You can find more about Noven Jaisi at:
www.novenjaisi.com

You can connect with him at:
Instagram: @novenjaisi
Facebook: @novenjaisi
Twitter: @novenjaisi

Notes

Notes

_____

_____

_____

_____

_____

_____

_____

_____

_____

_____

_____

_____

_____

_____

_____

_____

_____

_____

Notes

_____

_____

_____

_____

_____

_____

_____

_____

_____

_____

_____

_____

_____

_____

_____

_____

_____

Notes

_____

_____

_____

_____

_____

_____

_____

_____

_____

_____

_____

_____

_____

_____

_____

_____

_____

_____

_____

_____

Notes

Notes

_____

_____

_____

_____

_____

_____

_____

_____

_____

_____

_____

_____

_____

_____

_____

_____

_____

_____

_____

_____

Notes

Notes

Notes

Notes

_____

_____

_____

_____

_____

_____

_____

_____

_____

_____

_____

_____

_____

_____

_____

_____

_____

_____

_____

Manufactured by Amazon.ca
Bolton, ON